pumpkin chic

COUNTRY LIVING

pumpkin chic
decorating with pumpkins and gourds

principal photography by Andrew McCaul

principal styling by Lauren Hunter

text by Mary Caldwell

HEARST BOOKS
A DIVISION OF STERLING PUBLISHING CO., INC.
NEW YORK

Produced by Smallwood & Stewart, Inc., New York City

Editor: Bruce Shostak
Designer: Linda Kocur

Acknowledgments
The creative team would like to thank Thomas and Terri Holmes of Holmquest Farms, Hudson, New York; Mary Mullane; Warner Johnson; and Craig Fitt.

All photography by Andrew McCaul, except for the following: pages 4-5 and 17 by Roy Gumpel; page 7 (middle) and 56 by Keith Scott Morton; pages 8, 10, 21, 25 (bottom right), and 82 by Steven Randazzo.

Library of Congress Cataloging-in-Publication Data
Available upon request.

10 9 8 7 6 5 4 3 2 1

First Paperback Edition 2005
Published by Hearst Books
A Division of Sterling Publishing Co., Inc.
387 Park Avenue South, New York, NY 10016

Country Living is a trademark owned by Hearst Magazines Property, Inc., in USA, and Hearst Communications, Inc., in Canada. Hearst Books is a trademark owned by Hearst Communications, Inc.

www.countryliving.com

For information about custom editions, special sales, premium and corporate purchases, please contact Sterling Special Sales Department at 800-805-5489 or specialsales@sterlingpub.com.

Distributed in Canada by Sterling Publishing
℅ Canadian Manda Group, 165 Dufferin Street
Toronto, Ontario, Canada M6K 3H6

Distributed in Australia by Capricorn Link (Australia) Pty. Ltd.
P.O. Box 704, Windsor, NSW 2756 Australia

Printed in China

ISBN 1-58816-296-6

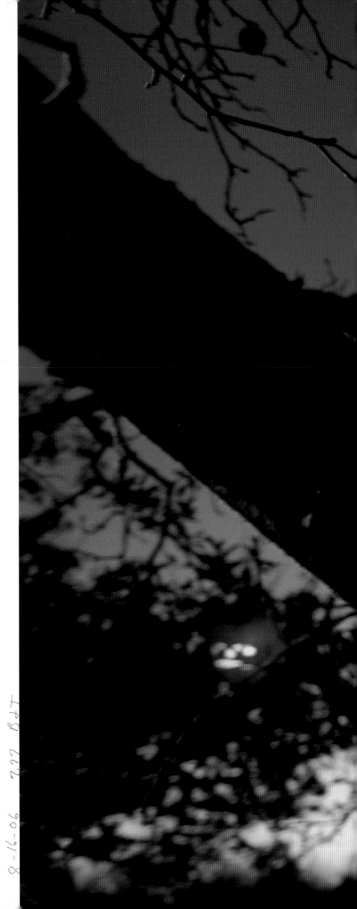

contents

introduction

What gives us joy in autumn, that season of colorful change, is that there's magic in it. The first flash of crimson leaves on a country lane, the excitement of planning a Halloween costume, and, yes, that first small orange pumpkin carried home from a market—maybe just a little bit too early for carving, but who can resist? These are the sweet highlights that capture the spirit around us.

This book is all about making the most of that pumpkin—and all of its squash and gourd cousins—in your seasonal decorating. Included are many inventive, out-of-the-ordinary jack-o'-lanterns. But here, too, are sophisticated and unusual ideas for using the farmstand's bounty to imbue your home with beauty all season long. Many pumpkins are illuminated from within, many etched only on the surface; some are so easy you'll want to launch an assembly line, while others take a bit more patience to complete. At the top of each project page, we indicate the spirit of the project: "quick concept" (truly *un*complicated), "artful touch" (adaptable and requiring some patience), "sum of its parts" (assembled materials), "uncarved features" (little or no carving required), and "autumn chic" (as at home in the city as in the country). Whether you choose to create a spooky pumpkin creature or a stylish gourd lantern, do read the first chapter, "The Basics," before digging in. We hope you'll be inspired to decorate, entertain, and celebrate with wonderful new twists on pumpkin carving and to create your own style of pumpkin chic.

the basics

The carving of the jack-o'-lantern has long been a Halloween custom in households where there are children, and with the increasing popularity of Halloween celebrations, the ritual is shared by adults and children alike. Beyond being transformed into jack-o'-lanterns, members of the viny genus *Cucurbita*—which includes pumpkins, gourds, and squashes—make wonderful decorating materials for the entire house, indoors and outdoors.

Legend holds that the Irish get credit for the jack-o'-lantern. Though renditions of the tale vary, it seems our grinning Jack evolved from lanterns carved out of turnips and carried in Celtic celebrations of the Day of the Dead. In recent years, pumpkin carving has evolved from crudely cut faces to sophisticated, intricate designs that are just as likely to become the centerpieces for a lovely dinner party as they are to liven up a round of trick or treating.

choosing what to carve

Pumpkins, the most traditional choice, range in size from the orange 'Jack Be Little' and the white 'Baby Boo' (each of which grows to no more than about three inches wide and two inches tall) to the mammoth prize-winning 'Atlantic Giant,' which can weigh in at over a whopping one thousand pounds.

The familiar orange pumpkin, a perennial favorite, is only one possibility for carving or decorating. Experiment with bumpy gourds, shapely speckled goose-necks, lantern-shaped specimens, and the Hubbard squash, whose ghostly green skin reveals a bright orange flesh.

But that's just the beginning. 'Kuri,' 'Kabocha,' 'Hokkaido,' 'Cushaw,' 'Lakota,' 'Delicata'—what sounds like a magical incantation is just a partial list of the many varieties of squash that are readily available today, joining the likes of acorn and butternut and the whimsical-sounding sweet dumpling. (All pumpkins and gourds are, technically, squashes.)

Hard-skinned winter squashes and gourds, such as acorn and butternut, require a bit more patience to carve, especially if the surface is prominently ridged or warty, but they can yield bewitching creations. Consider some of the stranger-looking species, too—for instance, the gooseneck gourd or the bumpy, pale blue-green-skinned Hubbard squash. Species with contrasting colors of skin and flesh, such as the white 'Lumina,' with its orange interior, will unleash the artist in you.

For best results, choose a specimen that has no soft spots or signs of mold or rot. Even if you intend to remove the stem, it's best to purchase a pumpkin with an intact stem, as the flesh is subject to quicker decay once the stem is broken. (To avoid accidents, never use the stem as a handle.) You don't necessarily need a "perfect" shape, however; surface bumps and quirky contours can all become integral to your design. Don't worry about caked-on dirt, either. Much of this can be easily removed with a stiff-bristled brush, a dampened sponge or rag, or a quick rinse under water.

planning the design

Pumpkins, squashes, and gourds hold practically unlimited potential for autumn and Halloween decorations. Go to the pumpkin patch with a design in hand and choose a

illuminating ideas

When lit from within, a jack-o'-lantern's persona emerges. Even the simplest designs look magical glowing in the dark, and any little "mistakes" will no longer matter.

candle power

Use candles safely. Place them only in steady pumpkins that won't be bumped or pose a hazard to children. A votive candle in a glass holder—or more than one, for brightness—or a taper candle that's become a bit stubby are the most reliable choices. To anchor a taper, scoop out a hole, drip a little melted wax into it, and immediately stick the candle in to secure it. Another trick is to cut a hole in the bottom of the pumpkin and slide the pumpkin over a candle. Light candles with a long fireplace match or a long electronic lighter.

electric power

A small flashlight or battery-operated pumpkin light (available with a steady or blinking beam) is a safe flame-free alternative; for a brighter glow, use more than one. You may wish to set the light on a square of folded plastic wrap to prevent it from becoming slimy.

Plug-in electric options include 25- to 40-watt bulbs in outdoor utility light sockets (great for thick pumpkins that need stronger illumination) and strands of outdoor Christmas lights (with these, you can create a pathway of luminaria). Choose red or green lights instead of white for extra eeriness. The new indoor/outdoor LED (light-emitting diode) strings of lights work well, too. To keep lights clean, cut the pumpkin's opening in the bottom and carve a narrow channel in the back of the base to allow the wire to escape without being pinched.

For lighting a pumpkin-filled porch, you can keep it classic with lanterns or hanging strings of carnival lights. For a jollier touch, especially great for kids, invest in strings of lights with bulb covers shaped like pumpkins or ghosts.

Carving a host of Halloween ghouls (opposite) might take several carvers several hours; if you choose a sole pumpkin, remember that the larger it is, the greater the effort and time required to prepare and carve it. For the work, kitchen knives and sturdy spoons are longtime standbys. Some other tools (top, left to right): potter's loop, chisel, awl, melon scoop, citrus zester, keyhole saw, apple corer, punch prick, and grapefruit knife. And other essentials (bottom, left to right): bamboo skewers for connecting parts, towel and brushes for cleanup, ice-cream scoop and pet-hair shedder for interior scraping, masking tape and china markers for outlining designs, and gardener's soil scoop for removing seeds and pulp.

suitable "canvas," or work the other way around and let the shape and character of a squash inspire you.

For freehand work, sketch the design onto the surface of the pumpkin. A china marker (grease pencil) or a gel pen works especially well for this task: Both write smoothly on the surface; any remaining traces can be wiped away with a damp cloth when you're done. You could also use a pencil, a ballpoint pen, or any pointed tool to etch the design in the surface. If you're using a paper stencil or template, tape it to the pumpkin and make a dotted outline in the skin with a pointed tool. Remove the paper and connect the dots as you carve.

gathering your tools

While pumpkin-carving tool kits are available commercially—at various levels of quality and cost—you can assemble a set to suit your personal preferences. You probably have almost everything you'll need in your toolbox and kitchen drawers. Numerous artists' and gardeners' implements can also be pressed into service. Experiment to see what works best for you.

An access hatch in the back of the pumpkin instead of a cut-out lid leaves the front of the pumpkin looking smooth; the notch eliminates guesswork when replacing the door. A chimney vent that was power-drilled with a hole-cutter drill bit near the top lets candle smoke and heat escape.

Here are some suggestions for what to try:

◆ for making cuts, a sharp paring knife, a thin boning knife, a curved-blade grapefruit knife, a utility knife, or a narrow serrated pumpkin saw; whichever you choose, remember that sharper is better—you won't have to apply as much pressure

◆ for chiseling, a wood-carving tool, sculptor's tool, or even a flat-head screwdriver

◆ for removing seeds and pulp, an ice cream scoop, serving spoon, potting scoop, or even a looped and serrated pet-shedding blade

◆ for making chimney vents and decorative holes, an electric drill and an apple corer

◆ for etching and inscribing, a citrus zester, linoleum cutter, or potter's tool

getting under way

Pumpkin carving is a messy business, but well worth it. Cover tables with newspaper and put out bowls or plastic bags to collect seeds, pulp, and carvings. As many veteran pumpkin carvers have found, precise chiseling and etching work is often easiest with the pumpkin resting steady in your lap; protect your clothing with a large utility towel.

For a pumpkin that will be illuminated from within, start by cutting an access hole. The traditional method is to carve a cap around the stem; it's easiest if you make an angular (e.g., octagonal) rather than a circular cutout. To prevent the cap from falling into the pumpkin, slant the cuts inward so that the lid will be wider at its top.

Another way to make an access hole is to cut a door in the back of the pumpkin, which leaves the front and top free for carving. Cut a door large enough for removal of the pulp

Once you settle on the most comfortable tools and apply a few cutting techniques, pumpkin carving lets you unleash your creative genius.

and the seeds, incorporating a notch in one side of the door so it will fit easily, like a puzzle piece; again, slant the cuts inward so the outside of the door is bigger than the inside. You may need to secure a back door in place with one or two toothpicks, floral u-pins, or cotter pins. If outdoor electric lights will be used, carve away a notch to leave a channel for the cord.

Hollowing out the pumpkin from the base suits some designs. The virtue of a base opening is that you can set the cut pumpkin directly over the lit candle instead of having to reach inside with a match; just be sure to protect surfaces against damage from the moist pumpkin.

Next, you'll need to clean out the inside of the pumpkin thoroughly. An ice cream scoop or a soil scoop manages the task well. If you wish, save the seeds, rinse them free of pulp, and roast them for a snack (recipe on page 87).

If you're going to burn a candle inside the pumpkin, you'll probably need a chimney vent for the escape of heat and smoke. Cut a triangular notch from the lid or, if you're using a back door or a base opening, a round hole behind the stem near the top of the pumpkin. For cutting chimney vents (or decorative holes) in pumpkins, an apple corer usually works fine. Use an electric drill fitted with a regular or hole-cutter bit to make quick work of multiple pumpkins and gourds that have very hard skin and flesh. Drill bits in various sizes will give you creative flexibility. Always wear protective goggles and exercise caution when drilling. Be sure the pumpkin is steady at all times.

Many designs call for scraping or chiseling away just a bit of the pumpkin, not cutting all the way through. This technique yields beautiful results that can be romantic or a bit spooky. If you're lighting a chiseled creation from the inside, you'll usually need to scrape away additional flesh from the inside of the pumpkin, making a thinner wall that reveals more of a glow.

Because most carving tools are basic and personal preferences abound (the same effect can be created using various tools), the instructions in this book list only the materials; specific tools or types of tools are suggested within the step-by-steps. Most projects can be adapted to various squashes, sizes, and interpretations, so feel free to use imagination and creativity as your guides.

In pumpkin carving as in food preparation, a sharp knife is always safer than a dull one because less pressure is required to make a sure cut. Always work slowly and carefully; pull the blade out of the flesh and reinsert it at the new angle when changing your carving direction.

chapter 2

Creatures

scary and nice

Come October, when it's time to venture out to the pumpkin patch or browse a local farmstand, unleash your imaginative powers as you select the squashes to put on your operating table. Exactly what—or maybe even whom—does a particular pumpkin remind you of? Not that pumpkin-picking has to turn into an identification exercise, but an open-minded look at autumn produce may suggest a new world of scary, winsome, or amusing characters.

Start by looking beyond those perfectly round orange pumpkins. Lopsided and warty-surfaced specimens can become jack-o'-lanterns with distinctive personalities. White- or green-skinned pumpkins and all manner of hard-shelled winter squashes give you the chance to create otherworldly characters.

For beginners, a good choice is the triangle-eyed, maniacally grinning jack-o'-lantern. It certainly holds a place of honor in the pumpkin hall of fame. Straight lines and simple shapes, after all, are the easiest to execute. Without too much more effort or skill, however, you can easily carve or assemble innovative creatures that will elicit lots of smiles or shrieks—and compliments.

No rule says that a pumpkin must sit upright, presenting a face on its broadside and a curled stem for its topknot. Tip the pumpkin on its side and

Get in a ghostly spirit with classic jack-o'-lanterns, rakishly decorated stem-nosed imps, and a complement of seasonal supplies: perhaps some twigs, seedpods, berries, sunflower blooms, or a faux crow. With luck, maybe a prowling cat will arrive to provide instant inspiration.

On Halloween night, pumpkins and gourds
may magically strive to animate themselves.
Help them along with a chisel and a cut or two.

the stem is suddenly, unmistakably, a funny nose. Or maybe that stem is a creepy tail and the base of the pumpkin is the area that deserves a face. Hang a pumpkin upside down: The stem is the neck of a ghoulish head. A squash could serve as the body of a creature, rather than its head, with sticks for arms and legs. Another option is to use the surface as a canvas: Carve the outline, silhouette style, of a bat, a cat, or a spider. Or try your hand at an old-fashioned silhouette of a family member or ancestor.

Seasonal materials can also enhance the personality of your creation. Ears of Indian corn, strands of ivy, and other ingredients can become fearsome facial features or a pumpkin fright wig. Ask yourself what role your pumpkin will play? Is it a bloodthirsty vampire? Frankenstein's monster? A wicked witch? A funny-faced sprite or a circus clown? Then ask yourself what different elements might become under your creative direction. Does a crooked chile pepper, turned sideways, look like a sinister leer? Do kernels of Indian corn resemble beady bat eyes. Props come in handy, too, especially at Halloween, when theatricality is the order of the day. Heighten the effect of a display with some treasures from the attic or toolshed. And now, let your pumpkin don its finery.

eerie props and spooky add-ons

For sly or spectacular effects, your jack-o'-lantern can be embellished in many ways other than carving. To involve children who are too young to wield cutting tools, you can, of course, let them paint their own designs on pumpkins large and small (or let them mark designs for you to cut). But with some extra elements you can really dress up your gourd.

theatrical spirit

Think in terms of wardrobe and props. Find a pointy witch's hat or a straw garden hat from summers past to lend sinister charm or rustic flair to glowing faces. Let a toy arrow or an old scythe inspire the setting of a grim and gruesome tableau, set up for a frightful Halloween fete. Use artificial—and surprisingly convincing—crows, bats, rats, spiders, and spiderwebs (widely available in the weeks leading up to the holiday) to stage a spooky show. You'd be surprised: Even a single uncarved pumpkin with a faux blackbird perched on its stem has the power to playfully startle visitors when they catch a glimpse through the front window.

natural weirdness

Look in the garden, yard, and woods and at floral shops, garden centers, and the grocery store for natural add-ons. Twigs are spindly arms or eerie antennae. Leaves or corn husks, attached with floral u-pins, can look like a ruffled collar or a shaggy coiffure. Seedpods, which nature offers in such astonishing variety, are abundant this time of year; use them as eyes, horns, or even tongues. Try sumac pods, pinecones, broom corn fronds, or cattails—just carve a hole into which the materials will fit snuggly. Even gourds themselves can be the add-ons. Don't be afraid to cut them apart to make eyes, ears, noses, or whatever else you can envision hiding in their round or coiled shapes.

scar-faced monster

No doubt a kin of Frankenstein's infamous creature, this not-at-all-handsome fellow is a frightful assemblage of parts—including his visible brain. To make one like him, select a large, squarish pumpkin, preferably with bulges and blemishes. This jack-o'-lantern requires only the most basic carving techniques—the misshapen add-on features provide the special effects.

1. Cut a door in the back of the pumpkin and scoop out the seeds and pulp. Cut a chimney vent behind the stem near the top of the pumpkin.

2. With a marker, sketch the eyes, nose, and mouth. Plan carefully so the round gourds will fit snugly into the eye sockets and the corn will fit into the mouth. Cut the eyes, nose, and mouth. With a citrus zester or a potter's tool, score two lines under one eye to suggest a black eye. Wedge in the gourd eyeballs. Remove several kernels from the cob to simulate missing teeth, then wedge it into the mouth opening.

3. Mark and cut a hole on one side of the forehead to accommodate the cockscomb "brains" snugly. Trim the stems from the cockscomb, then wedge the bunch into place.

4. For ears, cut the third gourd into quarters; clean out two of them. Insert two toothpicks into one cut edge of each "ear"; attach both to the head. Trim the toothpicks if necessary.

5. Insert the candle or light and replace the door.

materials

1 large pumpkin

several stems of cockscomb

1 ear Indian corn, trimmed to desired length

3 small round gourds

toothpicks or bamboo skewers

candle or battery-operated light

lidded flowerpot tableau

In days past, hollow dried gourds were pressed into service as water dippers. Freshly harvested winter squashes can be scooped out and filled with water to double as flower vases. Choose a variety of gourds and flowers to complement one another in a grouped arrangement. Here, from the left, are ornamental kale, calla lilies, and tulips—a flower-stall luxury this time of year.

1. Slice off the top inch or so of each squash, pumpkin, or gourd, cutting straight across, and save the lids. Remove the seeds and the pulp. Rinse out the interiors.

2. Fill each vase with water and arrange the flowers, one variety to each vase. To help keep them steady and to create a naturalistic scene, set the filled vases on a bed of moss and place the lids to the sides of the vases. If you wish, lay down a protective layer, such as plastic wrap, on the surface where you plan to set the grouping. To create a mess-free, movable tableau, fill a medium to large platter with moss and arrange the grouping on it.

materials

assorted pumpkins and winter squashes

flowering kale, calla lilies, and tulips, or other flowers

sheet moss or sphagnum moss

gourd-
topped
candelabra
With a little imagination, you can use a wide, flat pumpkin as the base for a dramatic and stylish candelit centerpiece. A creamy-colored specimen and a cascading pile of snow-white gourds hint at the approaching winter holiday season.

1. Carefully break or cut the stem off the pumpkin. Using a bit that's just a fraction smaller than the diameter of the candles, drill five evenly spaced holes in a ring around the top of the pumpkin, drilling straight down 1 to 2 inches.

2. Insert the candles into the holes; scrape the openings a tiny bit if necessary. If the holes are too big, secure the candle by wrapping the base with a strip of plastic wrap or a small amount of modeling glue.

3. Arrange the greenery on top of the pumpkin, allowing it to trail down the sides, and secure it in place with floral u-pins. Arrange the gourds on top of the greenery, securing each gourd to the pumpkin with a toothpick, if necessary, for stability. Set several gourds on the table, around the base of the pumpkin, to enhance the cascading effect.

materials

1 large flattish pumpkin

5 taper candles

seeded eucalyptus or other greenery

floral u-pins

toothpicks

assorted small white and pale-colored gourds

index